Lee Hoiby

ELEVEN SONGS

for MIDDLE VOICE & PIANO

ED-3974
First Printing: August 1995

ISBN 978-0-7935-4969-6

G. SCHIRMER, Inc.

DISTRIBUTED BY

HAL•LEONARD®

7777 W. BLUEMOUND RD. P.O. BOX 13819 MILWAUKEE, WI 53213

www.musicsalesclassical.com
www.halleonard.com

to Hans Leder

BEGINNING MY STUDIES

Walt Whitman

Lee Hoiby

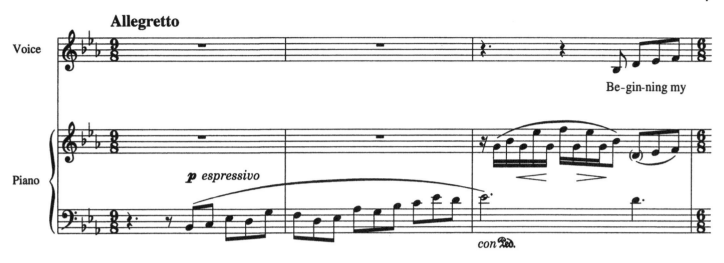

forms, the pow-er of mo-tion, the least ___ in-sect or

an - i-mal, the sen - -

- - ses, ___ eye - - - - sight,

love. ___ The first

step I say awed _____ me and pleased me so

much, I _____ have hard - ly gone and

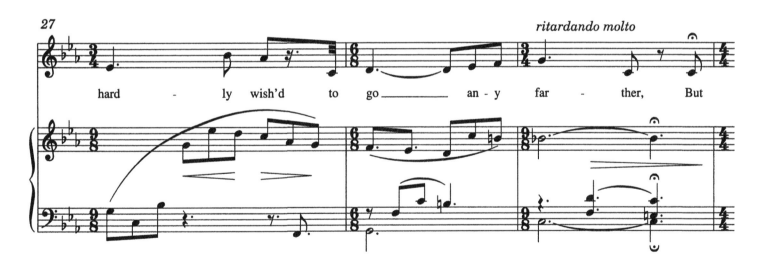

hard - ly wish'd to go _____ an - y far - ther, But

stop and loi - ter all the time to

4

to Michael Carson

A CLEAR MIDNIGHT

Walt Whitman

Lee Hoiby

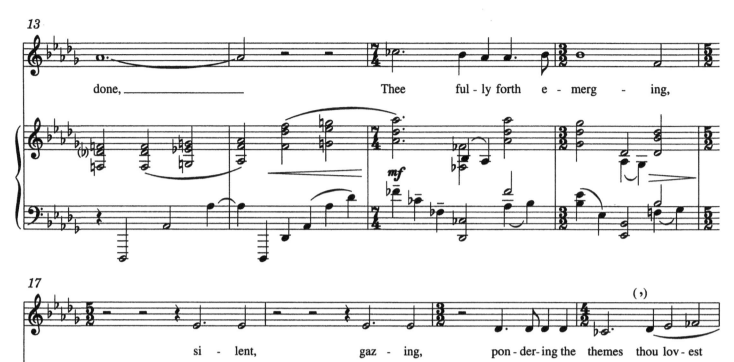

done, _____ Thee ful - ly forth e - merg - ing,

si - lent, gaz - ing, pon - der-ing the themes thou lov - est

Poco più lento

best, Night, sleep,

Tempo I

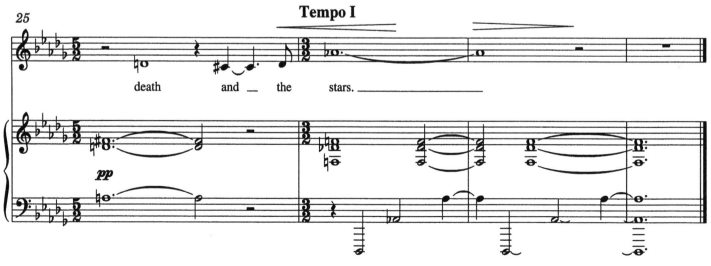

death and __ the stars. _____

to Paul C. Echols

JABBERWOCKY

Lewis Carroll

Lee Hoiby

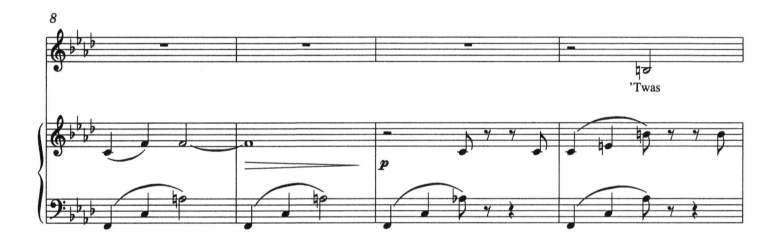

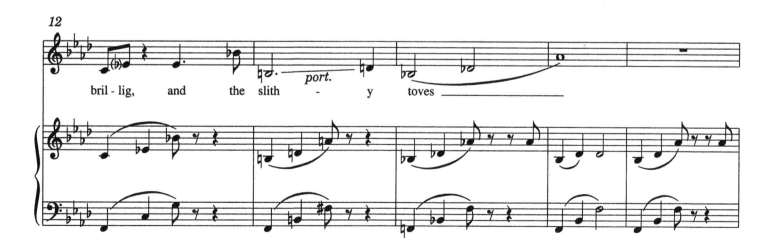

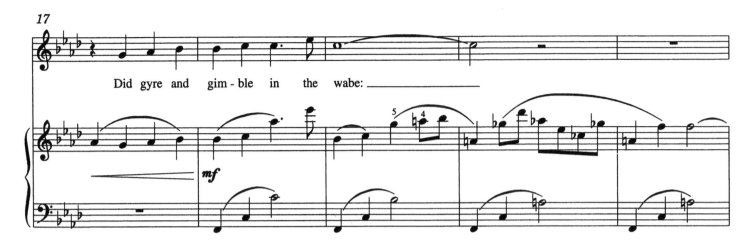

Did gyre and gim - ble in the wabe: _____

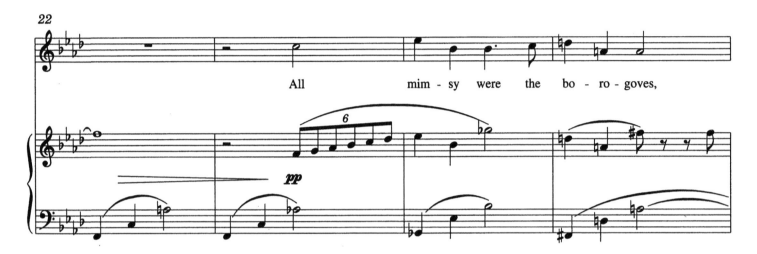

All mim - sy were the bo - ro - goves,

And the mome raths _____ out - grabe. _____

(darkly)

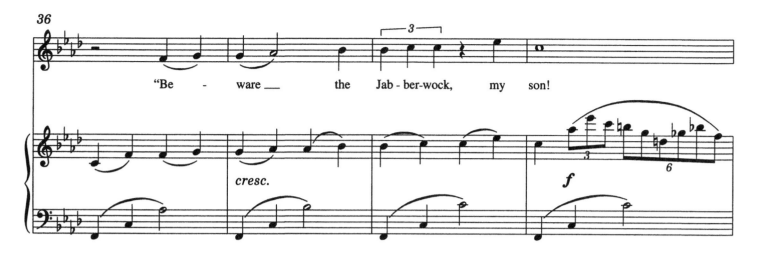

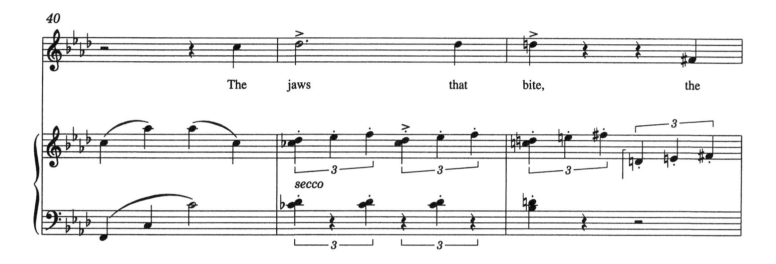

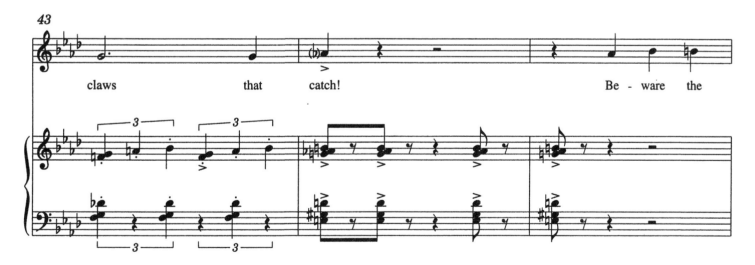

sought   So

rest - ed he by the Tum-tum tree, And stood a-while in thought.

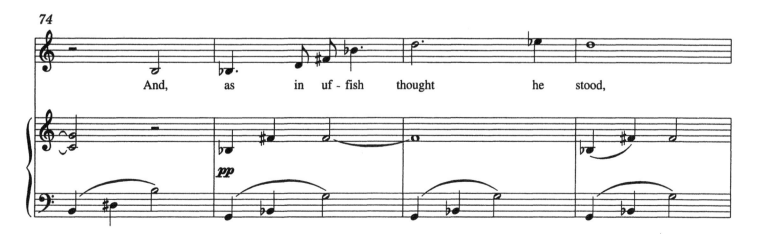

And, as in uf - fish thought he stood,

The Jab-ber-wock, with eyes of flame,

Came whif - fling through the tul - gey wood, And

bur - bled as it came! _____

poco allargando

a tempo, pesante

One, _____ two! _____

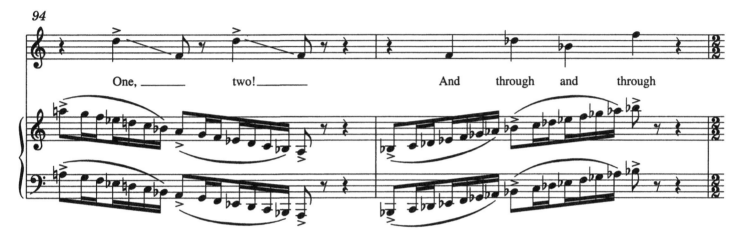

One, _____ two! _____   And   through   and   through

the   vor - pal   blade   went   snick-er - snack!   snick-er - snack!

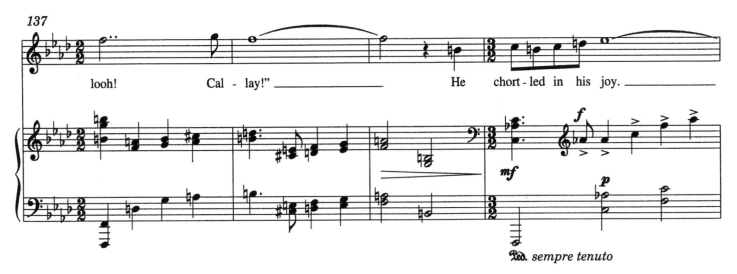

looh! Cal - lay!" _____ He chort - led in his joy. _____

Ped. sempre tenuto

Tempo I, misterioso

dim.

mp

pp

(*Ped.*)

'Twas bril - lig and the slith - y

port.

(*Ped.*) *

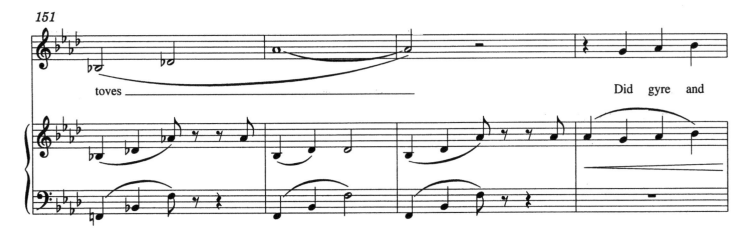

toves _____ Did gyre and

gim - ble   in   the   wabe: _____

All   mim - sy   were   the   bo - ro - goves,

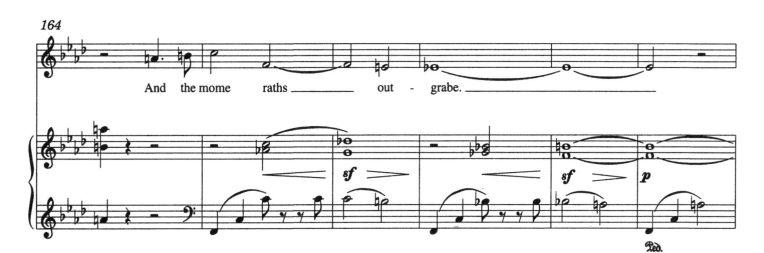

And   the mome   raths _____   out - grabe. _____

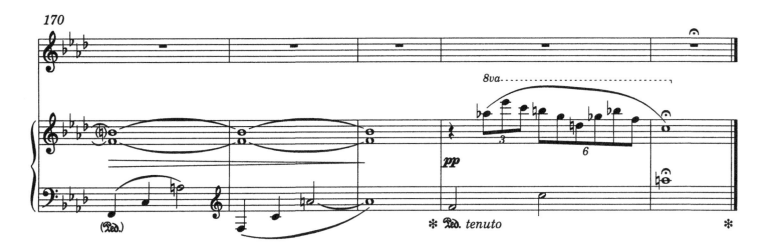

LADY OF THE HARBOR

Emma Lazarus

Lee Hoiby

I lift _____ my lamp _____

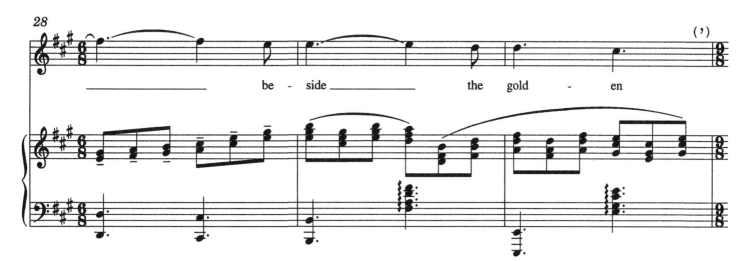

_____ be - side _____ the gold - en

door. _____

to Judith and John Saly

WHAT IF...

Samuel Taylor Coleridge

Lee Hoiby

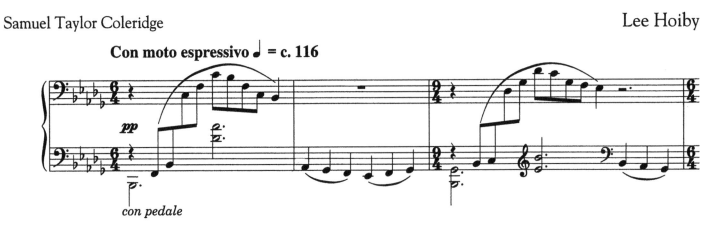

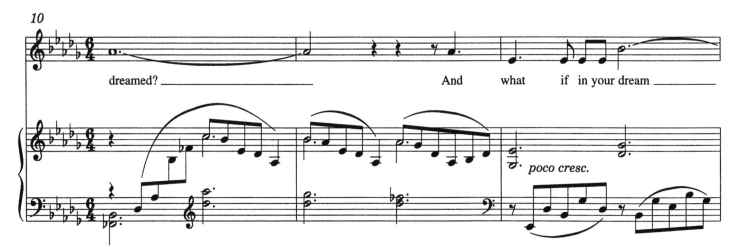

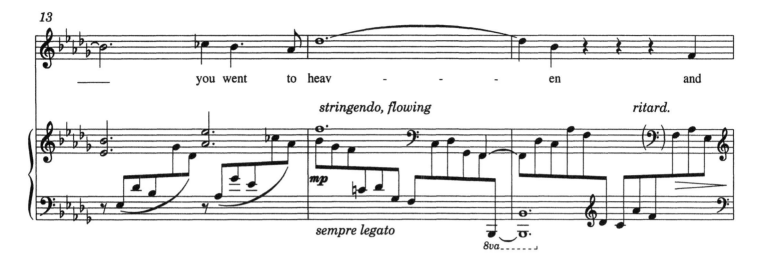

you went to heav - - - en and

there plucked a strange and beau - ti - ful flow'r?

And

what if when you a - wake, you had the

flow - er in your hand?

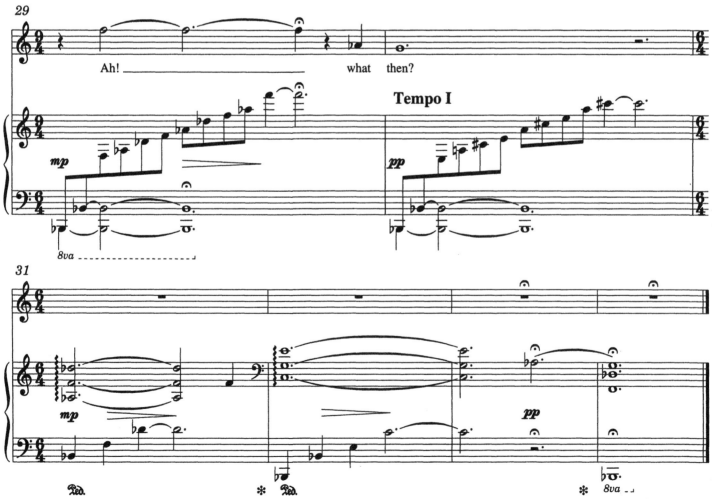

Ah! what then?

for Tom Fay

THE LAMB

William Blake

Lee Hoiby

meek and he is mild, He be - came a lit - tle child: ___

I ___ a child and thou ___ a lamb, We are

call - ed by his name. ___ Lit - tle Lamb, God bless thee.

Lit - tle Lamb, God bless thee. ___

for Olive Endres
THE SHEPHERD

William Blake

Lee Hoiby

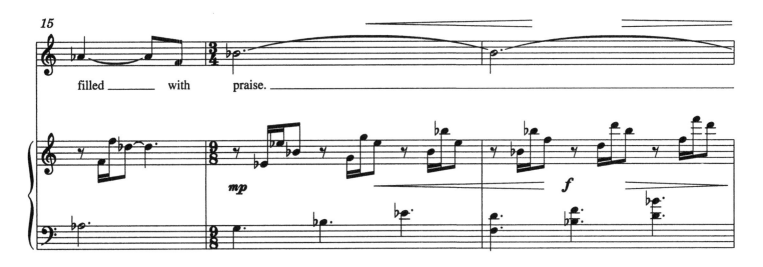

ten - der _____ re - ply. He is

watch - ful when they are in peace, For they know when their

shep - herd is nigh. _____

AN IMMORALITY

Ezra Pound

Lee Hoiby

SHE TELLS HER LOVE

Robert Graves

Lee Hoiby

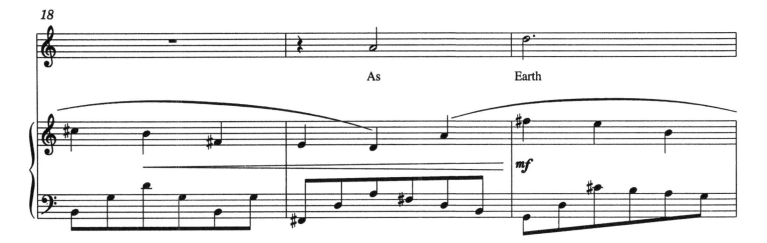

As Earth

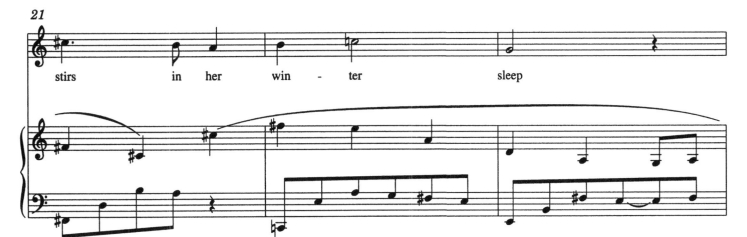

stirs in her win - ter sleep

and puts out grass _____ and

flow'rs _____ de - spite ___ the

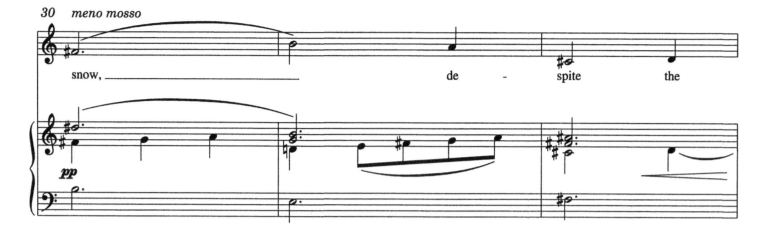

snow, _____ de - spite the

fall - ing snow. _____

to Lorenzo Malfatti

TO AN ISLE IN THE WATER

William Butler Yeats

Lee Hoiby

She car - ries in the dish - es, and

lays them in a row. To an isle in the

wa - ter with her would I

go.

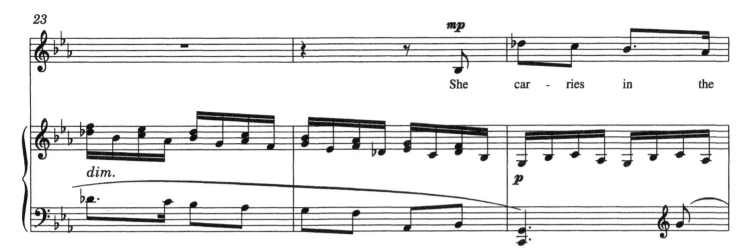

She car - ries in the

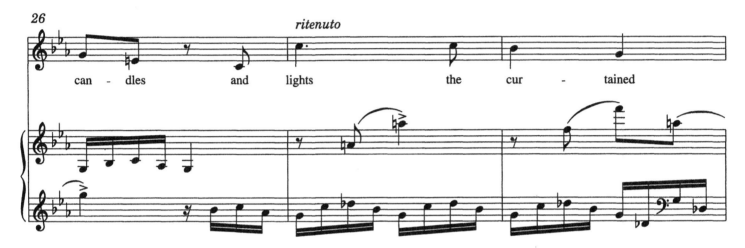

can - dles and lights the cur - tained

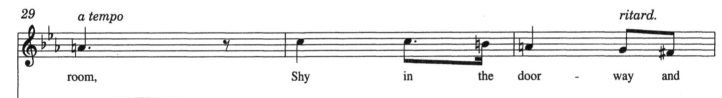

room, Shy in the door - way and

shy in the gloom;

to the Guide
WHERE THE MUSIC COMES FROM

Words and Music by
Lee Hoiby

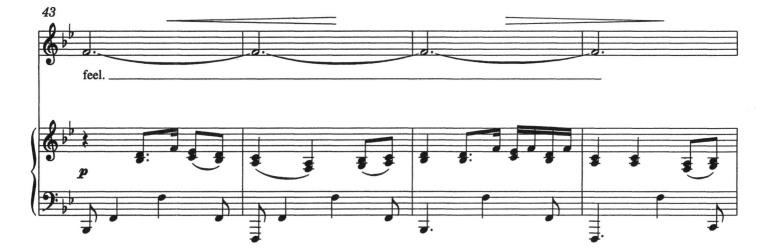

feel.

I want to

walk in the earth - ly gar - den, Far from cit - ies, far from

fear. I want to talk to the grow - ing gar - den, To the

* pronounced *day – vas* (nature spirits)